Praise for Strange Gift

With a keen eye for imagery, Veronica Kornberg brings the dearness of daily life to us from her perch on the edge of the Pacific, her newfound home: "We took it all on faith, as is. // Below us, the violent sea / broke its beautiful teeth on the rocks." Kornberg invites us into the rich sensory detail of the place and "how a person can be // changed entirely by the scent of sage and coyote mint, / by the quick tongues of painted ladies that swarm the sea daisies…" Against this backdrop, we're also led into family memories, "this conversation between the living and the long dead" and toward this conclusion: "It did not feel like loss, but a wheel turning." This is a lush debut, a narrative collection full of gift after *Strange Gift*.
—Ellen Bass, author of *Indigo*

Wondrous, dug from the earth, I trust these poems to lead me "toward the beat to follow, the flutter/ of blood, the bone."
—Danusha Laméris, author of *Blade By Blade*

Veronica Kornberg's gorgeous, transcendent poetry collection *Strange Gift* is a grounding, bountiful reaping—a landscape & seascape of memory which "peel[s] the body's waxy, rough skin / right down to the tender." These are some of the most distinctive, memorable poems on nature & memory that I've ever read. They never rush or push us into grief or joy. Instead, they offer us a sensory feast, a meditation on the tide, the garden & who we have loved & lost. *Strange Gift* is an elegant testament to "the hidden / marrow of days leaching thin." Alternating between vibrant & subtle images, these masterful poems remind me that being human means living in a shared world on borrowed time. And it is in that shared world that we must find ways to hold on, to let go & to bear witness to what remains.
—Joan Kwon Glass, author of *Daughter of Three Gone Kingdoms*

The world offers its gifts to us daily—strange, illuminating and sometimes comforting. In Veronica Kornberg's *Strange Gift*, you will enter a world within a world and recognize these luminous and curious offerings "in the billowed meadow of the night," along with "birdsong in the winter scrub,/wren-tit and fox sparrow." Kornberg has a detailed eye for the jewels and diamonds the natural world offers up in abundance but also for the discordant gestures of love revealed in one's own family, the on-going thrum of memories and the wonder of time. These poems remind us that if we pay close attention we too can stand "listening with our bodies" to "the rivers braiding inside us."
—Tina Schumann, author of *Praising the Paradox* and *Boneyard Heresies*

From the concrete edges of a New Jersey girlhood to the long-sought home on the Pacific Coast, the poems in Veronica Kornberg's *Strange Gift* trace a journey through landscapes that are at once external and deeply internal, ultimately a search for notions of home: "I thought maybe there was a place for me in this world," Kornberg writes in the titular poem, "a little side street off the parade route." In these poems, nature is both sanctuary and mirror reflecting the complexities of loss and renewal, a reminder that even in the most fractured and damaged landscapes, beauty persists. Above all, *Strange Gift* is a love letter to a life well-lived—to the bitter and the sweet, to loved ones past and present, and to the evening primrose in its unabashedly "frank availability." This is one stunning debut.
—Sarah Freligh, author of *Sad Math* and *Other Emergencies*

STRANGE GIFT

STRANGE GIFT

poems

Veronica Kornberg

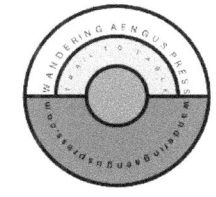

Wandering Aengus Press
www.wanderingaenguspress.com

Copyright © 2026 Veronica Kornberg
All rights reserved

This book may not be reproduced or transmitted in any form by any means, electronic or mechanical, including photocopying and recording, or by any information storage and retrieval system. Excerpts may not be reproduced, except when expressly permitted in writing by the author. Requests for permission should be addressed to the author at veronicakornberg@gmail.com.

Without in any way limiting the author's and publisher's exclusive rights under copyright, any use of this publication to "train" or develop generative artificial intelligence (AI) technologies is expressly prohibited. The author and publisher reserve all rights to license uses of this work for generative AI training and development of machine learning language models."

First edition

Poetry
ISBN: 978-1-966644-02-6

Cover Photo: Veronica Kornberg
Cover Design: Sophie Kornberg
Author Photo: Nada Nekrep

Wandering Aengus Press and its imprint Trail to Table Press
are dedicated to publishing works to enrich lives
and make the world a better place.

Wandering Aengus Press
PO Box 334, Eastsound, WA 98245
trailtotable.net
wanderingaenguspress.com

Contents

Bitter Greens	1

1.

Improvident	5
Beauty	7
Brogues	9
My Sister	11
Matisse in the National Gallery	13
Received Wisdom	14
Strange Gift	16
Home	17
Pair of Eyes	19
Graphesthesia	20
Winter Wallop	21
Strata	22
Rutabagas	23

2.

Stealing Mulberries	27
An Appreciation	28
Oysters	29
Seeds	30
Moon Garden	32
Sunday	33
Field Notes	34
Oceans of Time	35
What We Heard	36
Passion Flower	37
Stress Test	38
As If To Waltz	39
Gift Set	40
To An Oxbow Lake	41
Her Work	42
Stubborn	43
Morning Fog as Metaphor for Denial	44

3.

Apple Picking	47
Results Pending	48
Despite the Usual Traffic	50
Truth	51
Getting It Right	52
Fragment	53
Dear Thief	54
Age of the Romantics	55
A Daughter Leaves Home	56
The Work	58
Balloon	59
Ship Lights at Dawn	60
Sea Urchin	61
What the Ocean Dreams at Night	62
Heirloom	63
Hoshigaki	64
Farewell to Spring	65
Hidden Clock	66
My Soul Refuses to Write Itself	67
Soft Ground	68
Notes	70
Acknowledgments	71
Gratitude	73
About the Author	75

for Ken
&
for Jessie, Sophie, and Zoe

Bitter Greens

I know the bitter ones. The consonants that break
hard against the ear. Kale. Radicchio. Chard.
I know the dark billow of leaves, the wild ripple
above a cinch of twist-tied ankle stems,
the bulging veins in celadon or scarlet splitting
each one up the middle. I know the curly edges.
If they could speak, they'd sound exactly like
those cranky ladies slowly poisoning themselves
on front porches up and down Brenwall Avenue
in 1964. Hair sprayed in frozen waves or held in check
by nylon nets, rings of lipstick on the tan paper
of spent cigarettes scattered in an ashtray's upturned palm.
What does it mean, they asked, when the fanciest
house on the block got bought by a mixed-race couple?
We perched on the steps, watched their wagging
chins, their smoke rings. We waited for an opening
to beg for cookies. They almost always rose
from the sag of plastic lawn-chair webbing,
let the squealing screen door slam behind,
returned with chocolate chips or Oreos, those bitter,
house-coated women. We took their sweets and scrammed,
ran toward the thin patch of trees we called the woods,
toward the creek, the secret fort, the puddled
mosquito bog of dead man's lake. Ran
toward a future that didn't belong to them,
we thought.

1

Improvident

That dream, a small cottage
with windows facing the Pacific and
—wait for it—

priced within reason.
Of course
there were none.

So for twenty-five years we simply drove
the twisty mountain route
through a green welter of redwoods

to bottom out along the coast
among scattershot barns
and rusty propane tanks, happy

to end up at the state beach,
shield our ham and cheese
from sand-laced wind.

Eventually, our quest was more
idle banter than actual search
though we still nosed

into abandoned shacks
and tire-tracked lanes dead-ending
in junk heaps. What more could we want?

Until one foggy day, we spied
a peeled and faded sign set back
among overgrown cypress,

a footpath through a dense thicket
of dead pines that led to a cliff,
and perched on its crumbling edge—

a tiny house, crusted with orange lichen,
brown algae, and termite wings, the redwood
water tank staves bowed and bleeding water.

Within weeks, our nest egg was gutted,
We were out chopping dead trees
and fiddling with a pump bladder,

fielding chiropractors and pricing
used tractors. We chimed the names
of everything around us—

wrack line, blackberry, wentletrap,
wooly sea daisy and gumboot chiton.
We took it all on faith, as is.

Below us, the violent sea
broke its beautiful teeth
on the rocks.

Beauty

I spent Saturdays operating an elevator
in the last remaining department store
in downtown Trenton, a neighborhood
of singed bricks and boarded windows.
It was 1970. I was fourteen. A Dresden doll,
said one powdered woman to her friend.
I scissored the brass cage shut, thumbed
the button up or down. The days stretched thin
and hardly anyone came in.

I sang into the cavern of each echoing floor—
Fragrances, Men's Shoes, Lingerie.
Lanhn-ger-ray—so luscious, the tongue
lingering against the front teeth.

Reading was forbidden, so I taped a Cezanne
postcard above the red emergency button.
Something to look at. On his way up
to Customer Service, the manager said
to take the picture down. I stared implacably
at the blank green wall as he shifted
from one polished wingtip to the other until
the doors slung wide again, releasing him to plastic-
wrapped mattresses under fluorescent lights.

Late afternoons, the crossdressers appeared—joyful
angels in bright chiffon, cinched waists and man-calves
above sling-back heels, laughter rich and streaked
with ruby. A glued-on fingernail touching the corner
of a welling eye, thick-lashed and lined. Each week,
they teased, "Which floor for the Ladies Room?
Isn't it awful to get your period when you're not
expecting it?" I didn't have mine yet, but nodded
mutely, smoothed my skirt with sweaty palms. "Honey,
they cooed, "Don't *worry*."

Not long before I left for good, two women
rode with me in silence, standing arm in arm.
At the appointed floor, the doors stood wide
but they did not move. "Oh, ma," said one. "I wish
you could see this girl." She hesitated then,
"Do you mind if my mother touches your face?"
I stood still as a rabbit while the old woman's hands
found my temples. Flowery scent
on the cuff of her coat sleeve, the quick,
practiced touch over my cheekbones and chin.
"Beautiful," she said. Then in measured steps
they walked away and disappeared, taking
with them some version or vision of me
that had never existed before—someone, I kept
hoping, I could someday learn to be.

Brogues

Each Saturday night my father lined up our eighteen
        church shoes on newspaper pages on the dining room table,

opened his large tin of polishes, waxes, creams, and brushes,
        and set to work, smiling his private smile and whistling

through the wide gap between his front teeth. I kissed him
        goodnight to the scent of blacking.

He favored a shoe well-worn, patched
        and re-soled, the leather conditioned. *Boxcalf, full-grain, peccary.*

Cordovan, made of connective tissue from a horse's backside
        and come down centuries via the Spaniards of Córdoba. *Galoshes*,

wingtip, monk-strap—words delivered from his lips with pleasure and fanfare.
        Like the made-up nonsense words he roared

near nightly—as the toast burned or his *barouche* failed to start,
        as water rose through the basement floor or a ladder

tipped away from the window. *Brilt* he would yell.
        Brilt me back. Nipchule. We always laughed, but he

was nervous, with one malformed ankle, a limp, seven kids
        and a bad ticker. One evening he worried a hole in his pant leg

circling and circling one fingertip.
        When I lit out alone for California,

he stood in the driveway, holding my mother's elbow
        and a basket of items he thought I might need. I left

most of it with him—tiny prayer book, sewing kit, a bottle
        of Lily of the Valley.

He offered so much. I took so little. Years later, after he died,
    I carried home his black and white brogues, the old white polish

caked deep into cracks. Line of tiny holes along the toes and sides,
    swooping across the instep.

Brogues—for treading the boggy places,
    punched full of weepholes to let the water drain.

My Sister

The four of us—Kathie, Ruth,
our mom, and I—drove down
to Maryland to visit Annie
in the coma hospital where
she'd been sent after she
opened her eyes and moved
one finger. The place
was great—therapy
six hours a day and nurses
like strong, funny angels
swooping around her railed bed.
One terrifying thing—
every week, the team tested Annie
to see if she'd made
enough progress to stay
another week, and if she hadn't
she'd be moved elsewhere,
somewhere not so great
but nobody knew where.
There *was* no where. We should call
our congressman and tell him
to do something.

The day was bright
and cold. We wheeled Annie
outside and sat on a bench by
the parking lot, squinting into
the winter-low sun amid
pocked mounds of plowed snow
that had hardened to ice.
We chatted in Annie's direction—
about a cardinal in the naked dogwood,
about mom's poodle barking hysterically at
a snow woman in the yard,
about the balls of yarn slowly morphing
into a crocheted afghan on the recliner.

I heard us packing the silent spaces,
cramming them full of news and pictures.
Annie didn't have many words
but she could still make her famous
bird face to show a little sarcasm
so that made the conversation feel
familiar and less desperate. Annie began
to fixate on our mother. "She is scary,"
she stammered. A kind of miracle—
Annie speaking a complete sentence.
Our mother blanched,
then made a goofy-ugly face.
"Scary," she chimed, waving her
gloved fingers. It was the most
adult thing I've ever seen,
the way she swallowed that pain
and turned it into a sweet
lick of icing, a joke, a little nothing.
God it was awful.

Driving home, we stopped for the night
at a freeway motel, the four of us
in one room. In the lobby, we scarfed down
a buffet— honeyed ham
and gloppy macaroni salad,
dinner rolls spongey and soft as
an old man's belly. There were two double
beds in the room and when I plopped
on the corner of one, the whole mattress
flew up toward the ceiling in a way
that I cannot explain the physics of
to this day. But I kept doing it,
the mattress jackknifing in the dim room
until we were all laughing—
we laughed and laughed until
we cried we were laughing so hard.

Matisse in the National Gallery

The artist's wife leans on the turquoise
arm of a slat-backed chair. Her eyes swim—
two black fish in the glass bowl of her face.
The shoulders and sleeves of her blue coat
lose themselves to the background's indigo
swirls. From across the room, four goldfish
watch from a clear cylinder, their orange
reflections trapped on the water's surface.
They swim among rough approximations
of philodendron, nasturtium, elephant ears.
Captive within a painted matrix, all circle—
wife, fish, blossom, smudged muddle of
the left hand, the feather nodding on her hat.
In other words, nothing extraordinary—
A woman waits underwater. A fish swims
among houseplants. A girl in a museum sees,
forgets to breathe.

Received Wisdom

A horse fence
still standing despite
posts cracked and rotting at the core
posts thistled with nail heads
where various rails have fallen

woodgrain weathered
bitten deep into boards
silvery as flowing mane
and bearded with lichen
the colors of lime and cloud, turmeric

a bucolic image— but up close
the whiff of molder
in the bone dust acre

what is a horse fence anyway—
a nod of agreement
an arch of the neck

I knew a horse
who jumped a six-foot fence
for a patch of extra-green grass
then sated
jumped back in again

such amicability—
oh you
confounding horses of the mind
pied and dappled round-
haunched and supple

you ripple the rough sod
whicker salted air
and race the length
of the falling-down fence
yet fail to vault

even where the fence lies
in pieces you wait
at the imaginary edges
one hoof pawing the ground
dust drifting from your back

Strange Gift

Like when I crawled through the back of my mother's closet
to crouch in the cubbyhole above the eaves, a flashlight
strung from a rafter nail, and Emily Dickinson murmured
something to Joyce Carol Oates, then the rain started
finger-tapping and they both turned to gaze at me,
their severe middle-parted hairdos and questioning eyes,
the glint off a small gem at the neck, or maybe it wasn't rain at all
but the family hubbub from the rooms below, and I felt
a great set of wings settle overhead, a soft and living roof
and I thought maybe there was a place for me in this world,
a little side street off the parade route. It was quiet I craved,
and this conversation between the living and the long dead,
the burble of mourning doves, the pianissimo trill on a Goth
baby grand, I wanted to see all that the dark corners held,
the dead girls whispering under a porch, the shiny black gun.

Home

No matter how long I live here
I'll never be a local, always

someone from over the hill.
Never named queen

of the Chamarita, never read currents
as easily as the lines of my palm.

I settle into my secret cove, awaiting
the return of the elephant seals

who winter here. Each day the tide
steals my boot prints from the sand.

Each day I plant them new. The limit
per catch of giant owl limpet,

my neighbor says, is thirty-two.
Sautés up nice. Named

for an attachment scar
that looks like an owl

on the inside of the shell.
You can see it only if you shuck it.

The owl limpet tends its algal plot
on wave-wracked rocks

bulldozing barnacles
and baby mussels, then retreating

to its home scar—the precise hole
it's carved for itself in the rock.

If you pried me away from this place,
turned me over and gutted me

you'd find a picture in the shape of
a house, a wave the color of pearl.

If you held me to your ear
you'd hear the click of the perfect

match of key to latch.

Pair of Eyes

If I could steal just one thing from the Met,
ferret it away with no one the wiser, I'd pocket

the gaze of two eyes made of marble, frit, and obsidian
lashed with bronze and set to float like butterflies pinned

under glass in the Room of Antiquities. Steady.
Intent. As if never sundered or plucked from some stone-headed

god in a hilltop temple. As if still waking
to long rows of gnarled olives and Mediterranean light breaking

over karst cliffs, light washing into sea grottos.
One eye umbra, the other mint. The astonished O

of the iris, unblinked. An atheist in Catholic school,
I secretly added an extra o to God. *Good* was cool.

I was down with good. *Glory be to good.* I savored my extra
O, tucked like magic beneath my tongue, vexed

to be different, soothed to be hooped, my two selves unsintered.
O ancient eyes in your museum case—you who knows no splinter

in the mind, no crack in the column, despite a flawed
world long crashed—*draw me a sun soul. Draw me.*

Graphesthesia

This is how I learned
to love

words traced on my back
letter by letter
fingertip language of my sisters

the body a book
the body an ear
an amphora filling
a slate wiped clean

first an L—the quick plunge
and plank at the waistband
then O—bumping over
the shoulder blade

L… O…

was it LONG?
Was it LOW?
Was it LOOP?

Make it LOVE!
I begged
for the sweep of their hands
on the page of my back—

it was LOVELY.

Winter Wallop

The mountain fell into the road,
the road fell into the sea,
cypress fell along the fence line,
and I, into reverie. Blue
sailboat dissolving in haze,
scent of black sage on my sleeve,
rocks clacking in the backwash.
I fell into the romance
of everything changing.
The way California is always
shifting, cracking open new veins
of gold, grinding out high peaks.
It did not feel like loss, but
a wheel turning. I felt this
even as my friend
lingered in his blue cotton gown,
amid mists of antiseptic wash,
amid the mechanical whoosh.
Even then, I studied the landscape
and spoke of love
though love fell on me, like loss.

Strata

this house perched on the radical	osteoporotic latticework of pocked stone	below our feet here a bellows blows	new breath new fodder in the uplifted
cliff edge where a hungry sea	carves *tafoni* (from Greek for tombs)	honeycombs the great lungs of the earth	rooms of the dead where time
chews the Pleistocene matrix	salt weathered grottoed and gouged	carves *tafoni* (from Sicilian for windows)	makes clear that erosion opens up
gobbles the substrate to a filagree	each story and nook a home transformed	returning the relentless churn to	this house this breath this hunger

Rutabagas

Rude. Root. Bagel. Beg.
The violet rumps.
The creamy tips.
Warts, hairs, bumps, dimples.
The faint whiff of dirty diapers
as they cook. A swede, a neep,
a tumshie, a moot. I don't know why
I want rutabagas in my kitchen
this wintry night. Staple food
of the concentration camps,
food of last resort.
Original jack-o-lantern
carried through dark streets
by children, to ward off bad spirits.
Maybe it's the satisfaction I want,
to pare leaf scars from the neck,
peel the body's waxy, rough skin
right down to the tender.

2

Stealing Mulberries
after Robert Penn Warren

Walking, hungry, the concrete edge of girlhood,
Where sixteen-wheelers thundered diesel blast,
Road black as grackle, oil-slicked, dead wood
Bristling the stunted scrub — chafe-hearted, I passed
A clump of broad-leaved trees holding fast

To the cracked curb, the heaved slabs
Tilted and broken, sprouting soot-choked sowthistle
And cocklebur, the pocked concrete drab, dabbed
With purple splotch, ink-blot, clotted with a drizzle
Of fallen fruit-flesh. And looking up, I saw the colossal

Leaf-sea of a mulberry tree. Green, shimmering high,
High as the tangle of telephone lines, strung
With sun-bleached sneakers and wind-flung trash, high
As its blue lair, the shaggy green sky-beast lunged
After each passing truck, its thousand small black tongues

Beckoning, and so I placed my foot in the crook
And climbed, limb after limb, scraping
Knees and shins on the bark. Bark-shinned I shimmied,
Lusting after those sweet tongues, and escaped
Completely into the high branches— a green, leaf-draped,

World I wished never to leave. But of course I left.
With purple-stained hands, face, clothes, sated slack-brain,
Bird treble in my ears, I crossed Route 31, not yet bereft
Of a short, passing season, its unlocked sugar of sap and rain,
Not yet aware that the trodden path would lead me back again.

An Appreciation

This time, I took the window seat.
Awake alone in the darkened cabin,
I slid open the shade, to look for what you
had often marveled at—the aurora borealis
glamorizing the polar route.
But filling the entire frame instead, the dim
connect-the-dots of the Big Dipper.
Big deal. There had to be more!
I stared a while at the curved handle,
the squared-off bowl forever ladling
darkness. So this, I thought, is mine:
soup on a cold night: familiar tune
written on the staff of an empty ocean:
sleeping question mark of ordinary light.

Oysters

Waves and wind. Sea lather
jiggling among rocks or flung
to clear the cliffs and catch
on cypress limbs. The mind
swims slowly in its shell:

memories of last year
your chest sawn open,
the light pulled to a pinprick.
We are like oysters
the doctor said

our bodies layer a husk
around every point of irritation.
You have worried the grains
to a sunken treasure of pink
pearls where the knife entered,

veins fished from your leg,
the ribcage wired shut.
Remember now: summer
butter lupine, now: the sun,
coral nub plunging beneath fog.

Seeds

Sleek and fat
they hunkered
in the ribs

of their husk canoes.
In hulls they
floated

woozy on brown stalks
that bobbed in light
breezes. Bobbing

in light I plied
the dry sea
of stalks laden

with capsules ready
to split. I pried
each pod apart

let the seeds
drop into a brown
coffee filter

instead of earth
where they hoped
to become their late

blooming selves.
I hoped for
late blooming

myself, carried my own
vision inside
folded brown paper—

hallucinatory fields
of sage and sea thrift,
trumpets and landfall.

Moon Garden

The Evening Primrose is anything but
        prim. I blush at its frank availability—

the fleshy stigma, swollen and sticky, that reaches
        beyond a yellow hem of heart-shaped petals,

drool in the night air and sacs of scent pumped
        loud as house music. The smell of damp earth,

blood of the gods, rises under a ruddy buck moon.
        I wait for the arrival of a sphinx moth,

which I have never seen. I am not a true creature
        of the night. Not at ease with the beetle

laboring toward nectar glands, nor with globs of pollen
        dropped and drifting on ghostly sheets.

I draw my coat around my knees even as I whisper
        my poems to this floating world.

Sunday

You'll find me on my knees
in the barked clearing
beneath the cypress. Say late March,
when seedlings tessellate the ground.
I could be praying, only
in some personal religion
of weed management—
it's embarrassing,
the degree of pleasure taken
in the easing of an intact root
from the loam. That slight give
of the fleshy taper
glowing faintly
like an upside-down altar candle
pulled from the dark.

Sunday—with your great Pacific
sigh at the base of the cliffs, your seabirds
ratcheting the sun
down through the trees, with me
resting finally
in the hammock of your hand.

Field Notes
after Jericho Brown

In the billowed meadow of the night
A bobcat trots unseen between the sage and lupine.

      The soul hunts at night, smelling of sage and pine.
      I check the box. I am not a robot.

Outside the box—stories and dirt. Robotic
Surgery of the soul. I light the candles.

      In this anatomical theatre, I candle
      The egg, but the egg keeps its mysteries.

Who I am will remain a mystery.
I carry the entire throng of me

      Into each day. Is it wrong of me
      To say I am a six-fingered star,

A scalpel, a germ, a silent movie star,
A bobcat sleeping in the meadow of the night?

Oceans of Time

From Papa to Poppy, then Poppyseed
to Seed. And finally, to Weed.
That's what we called him—
Weed. A man with no money, seven kids,
and a lot of ideas. He had bad wheels,
meaning his feet. And an ocean
of waves on his head. Occasionally,
he weeded the tomato patch. Often, he knelt
among kids in the sandbox, bless him.

In the bathroom, I once saw him
rise from the tub like Poseidon from the ocean,
bathwater rivering down his torso. *Kiddoo*
he said, snatching a towel. *Kiddoo* I said back,
staring. Weed. What did he desire, beyond a night
out alone with my mother, her body
pressed against his?

And what do I want now, here
with the ocean pounding at a distance and yellow
poppies feathering up from the soil? I want his arms—
muscled arms to catch a cartwheeling
umbrella in the nick of time, or lift me high
on his shoulders as a wave overwhelmed him.
Weed—how I miss the name in my mouth.

A man of the gentle kidding kind,
a man lost to the ocean of time. My heart
wheels around the gone-ness of him.
It's him I want—my pops,
my poppy and I, his poppet.

What We Heard
after Ada Limón

All that birdsong in the winter scrub,
        wrentit and fox sparrow,
drab towhee under green tongues—

coyote mint, wild lilac.
        Listening, you say
it's like the sound of thinking.

Or camouflage, I say,
        the earth
masking its secret music.

Now we hear the freeway
        hum in the distance
and I remember our walk

on the salt flats in Death Valley,
        the silence there
huge and physical, pressing.

We heard nothing
        but our heartbeats, stood
listening with our bodies

to our bodies, the rivers
        braiding inside us, two
creatures under a wallop of sky.

Passion Flower

A matted dome of avid shoots and hot
pink stars, thirty feet high and wide as a house,
the vine entombs an entire stand
of myoporum trees, chokes their light.

We hack a human-sized hole
to access the dark vault
beneath the trees, and stand in silence,
letting our eyes adjust to the gloom, as in

a swift descent from midday's glare
to chapel crypt, earthy incense.
The old tree trunks rise around us,
columnar, ghostly, and we see

how woodpeckers have honeycombed
every barked surface and how
the high branches crush under the weight
of the vine's false canopy. And too,

we see each tree limb stippled
with small bouquets of green leaves
despite the dearth of light. We pause
to feel the magic here,

so brief. Then lift
the clippers and the blades, the folding saw,
to begin the work
of cutting toward a flood of sky.

Stress Test

Red is the crest of the purple
finch and raspberry red
my heart, a flittering hankie
snagged on pine branches

and long the song of the purple
finch, laddered long
like the stuttered start of the heart
just prior to rising

there in the sky, five purple
clouds warble in the darkening
inside me, an arpeggio
drawn from the cords

until silent, the long land and purple
trees all reaching, reaching
toward the beat to follow, the flutter
of blood, the bone

As If To Waltz

What are they thinking, the old he-lizards
with their lizard brains? Late October, but instead
of readying to hibernate, they're looking to get busy
with the she-lizards on the wall outside my writing shed.
Flashing cobalt bellies, strutting yellow thighs.
One long-tailed, puffed-up fellow pumped one hundred
push-ups in the waning autumn light. Does he not realize
the rain is nigh, the fox tucked inside her den?
Or like the poppy blooming out of season, does he rise
and fall in rhythm to our newly unwound clock? When
drought strains the olive trees until they split and crack,
when forests curdle brown and corals blanch, who then
in vanishing hours shall fault the maniacs
who dance, who mime a spell as if to waltz us back?

Gift Set

Yellowed nacre cover and chipped spine. A muslin hinge, exposed by design. Why did I choose her *Catholic Pocket Manual* as memento? Mostly hokum to me, all capitalized pronouns and Penance, power moves over the lives of women. My sister says our mother carried it up the aisle on her wedding day, part of a bridal gift-set with matching comb and hair brush. Hah! A perfect token of that mind-fuck label *demi-vierge*. For sixty years, the comb and brush took pride-of-place atop her dresser, but the book lay nestled beneath silk scarves in her lingerie drawer, like a blocky yellow tooth or lady's pearl-handled gun. Yet, she must have held it in her hands, the shell cover cool and smooth and dangerous beneath her fingertips. A satin ribbon marks her last chapter—"The Examination of Conscience." What had she to repent, my strict, loving mother? When I fan the pages now, the scent of talcum makes me sneeze. How many times can I open the book before the perfume fades?

To An Oxbow Lake

You—born of a river's tendency
to meander through flatlands—
your quiet
silt-root heart and rubbery
green leaves.
Little mud island in the middle.
Twig nests wedged
among branches above the waterline.
No matter you're called
bog, mosquito trap, quagmire—
for me you will always be
the singular place, closed off
from the running stream,
sound of evening wingbeats
coming to roost, soft puffery
of down over brown-speckled eggs.
Pinks and golds sliding
between deep shadows.
I know you are meant
to disappear. To fill and solidify
into dirt and grasses.
I listen to the glop and ripple
of bluegills mouthing water skaters,
the rattle of dabbling ducks.

Her Work

From the bone to the broth, the hidden
marrow of days leaching thin, from a wind-whack
of pie plates on bean and tomato vines,

from hand-sewn nights, threads knotted and bitten,
work of her hands, the kneading, the whipping
of cream for a cake, quick chop

of the knife, quick check down the list, scrape
of the chair as she rose, kiss on the hair,
swipe of cloth in the soft nick of the jaw,

until deep in the evening she finally sat with her cup
of Red Rose, feet puffy and propped on a kitchen stool,
the Trenton Times unread in her lap as we ciphered

our long division and the rule of the run-on sentence,
while stock thickened in the pot and the next day's dough
swelled beneath flour sack towels and we settled, hungry
for the bread of her voice.

Stubborn

I like a spring that will not sing,
a spring that hoards tall stacks

of mountain snow and won't let go,
a spring that fills the village streets

with hungry bears that cannot glean
a single blade of tender grass beneath the snow.

There is a wide-stanced ice-capped
mountain in me that will not yield,

will not let loose the wild waters
to thirsty fields nor fill the falls.

What to make of such a mass
immovable? Was it born or built?

The mountain stands at the center
of the picture, listening through snowdrifts.

Morning Fog as Metaphor for Denial

Spring set you down
on the bluff, a blindfold

on the face of the day—
white noise, fur

and salt, shaggy giant
breathing over the deep.

Sweep your grey
beard through salvia,

gooseberry and aster,
dampen the croak of the waking

heron as a gathering blue
riddles your back, an upwelling

of cold your belly.
This is the pause

just before you burn.

3

Apple Picking

In the photo my mother stands among branches
in the orchard, holding an exquisite ripe globe
in front of her chest. She squints into sharp sunlight,
eager to tell me, behind the camera, the importance
of where on the tree to find the best, which to leave,
how to twist each apple upward for a clean stem snap.
She is eighty-nine at the time, vigorous, a halo
of white hair, in lipstick and a striped sweater set.
Her sit-down walker is off between trees, out of view,
tilted on the uneven ground as though she leapt up
out of it, tossed it aside. I want to say she looks like
an aged Eve in Paradise, but my mind harkens
instead to a summer in Lecce, the heel of Italy's boot,
to all those baroque churches covered in carved
stone vegetables and pomegranates, birds and putti,
where painted wooden saints rush from their niches,
polychrome in fervid blues, browns, reds.
Those saints! How I loved them. How they strode forth,
each holding in its hand its own pierced red heart
in panic or offering or love,
each heart astonished, ablaze in gold-leaf flames.

Results Pending

My dog lifts her nose to the wind. Spine fur spikes from the root.

The ancient stone carvings at Monte Alban— *Dancers*— are renamed *Captives*.

Take a moment. Pretzel your body. What do you call yourself now?

Beached sequoia, big as a whale, flamboyant knot like an eye tilting skyward.

Image may contain: 1 person, spume, power tool, indoors, and close up.

I want to see the Botticelli hair of that girl gliding toward me in a convertible.

Instead, my mouth fills with sardines.

I skipped alongside my father, pigtails flying. When I reached up, it was not his hand.

An orchestra with no string section plays Dvorják's *New World Symphony* in the town square.

30 miles south, orcas feed on whales; mothers teach their young to hunt calves.

It could be bad. Or maybe hyacinths, like fragrant bruises.

I like dancing but only when I feel safe, which is almost never, despite the candles.

Leviathan? No, *God*. I trusted all of it. Now I drink my coffee cold.

No signpost, but this wind tells me of a road that leads to a different country.

Despite the Usual Traffic

Divers haul up a lost city from the seabed—stone heads and torsos, inscribed slabs.

Elsewhere, radioactive grasses swallow a parking lot full of abandoned cars.

I've a mind of medieval streets tonight, cobbled warrens twisting under the pressure of a moonless lid.

My bones are not the bones of the dead, the femur lengthens, expands, compresses with each step.

The stucco walls, dotted with flowerpots, spout words in a new language.

A little horse pulls its load of tourists uphill. Only the harness wonders why.

Truth

A half-dozen small black fish, circling
in the tidepool. I reach to catch one
only to realize the real fish,

translucent as mucilage,
are swimming at the surface.
I've been watching their vivid shadows

cast upon the sandy bottom—
the silhouette more compelling
than the real. Neuroscience

says no sooner does a neuron snap
than narratives begin to populate the mind.
We all want to grasp the slippery

undulating truth. I cup
my hands at the tidepool's bottom,
wait for a fish to enter,

and the impossible black sculpin
wavers onto my palm. I feel it lipping
my lifeline, my submerged chalice.

Getting It Right

Suppose a woman never once scratched at her neck in night's purgatory

listing each minor misstep in the evening's conversation—calling the stemmy plant

broom instead of rush, mincing a precise explanation of LDL versus HDL when Essie

got it wrong, then forgetting her mother was sick. Suppose

she could fall into sleep like a stone toppled in meadow grass and poppies.

Mostly, she was solid. Like once, when sitting by the bed of a friend who was dying,

the hospital chaplain turned to her and asked what she believed in. *The primacy of human dignity.*

But suppose a grown woman had never told her mother that a man in the living room

once fingered her breast buds? Suppose her mother hadn't retorted, *well why did you let him?*

Suppose a child could explain that she'd done nothing wrong.

Suppose she could explain things very well.

Suppose it mattered.

Fragment

I peer beneath your bed for teeth and find slippers stinking of old piss.

Half-eaten cookie, wadded tissues, melted tube of Coral Sunset.

There— fragment of your smile, crescent of tombstones on a pink hill.

That's not possible, you say. How to help you

make sense of a world where things appear and disappear so

randomly. Guess the tooth fairy didn't want them.

Your eyes gleam. Wind wakes leaves and litter in a gray tunnel.

Your cousin's red hair: flame in the cornfield.

Hydrangeas blushing hyacinth in a lost summer. Long ago,

your whole house burned to the ground.

I fold stained slippers into the trash, rush out to buy two new pairs.

But your right foot is swollen as a sausage, drags

when you walk and knocks the slipper off. My flight is due.

You lean on the doorframe, smiling: See you tomorrow. In two months, Ma,

two months. I'll mail more slippers. I imagine shoeboxes

arriving from the blue, the way you'll cock your head

as the aid lifts them for you to see. Ancient chickadee.

Wave. It was lovely to see you, as though we're old friends, met for lunch.

        I become another thing that has appeared, disappeared.

Dear Thief

You jimmied the lock on my brain,
slid open the window and climbed inside.

Now I can't unsee you, lounging on that kilim
I bought in Istanbul in the 90's, smoke

from a hookah wreathing my antique cartoons
of scientists: Pasteur cradling a rabbit,

Curie raising a vial of polonium
as if toasting with a champagne flute, her eyes

yet to be scarred by radiation. So odd to find myself
hoping my flannel pajamas fit you,

that your toes are long and beautiful, your nails
coated with the purple lacquer you nicked.

The police want a detailed list of losses
and values. How much is a kindergarten

watercolor worth? A whale's vertebra dragged up
from the beach? Whitman said *nothing is ever really lost,*

or can be lost, but I don't know. I press my hand
to the dark rectangle on a sun-bleached wall.

Age of the Romantics

Old wooden bench with a crude rose
carved on the back and toothmarks
along one armrest—testament to boredom
on the part of our long-deceased beagle.
This is supposed to be a poem about
the bench, which I placed so recently
in the secluded little arbor under the myoporum.
But here comes Boots, trotting into view.
Tongue out, hitch in the rear leg, gray muzzle.
Here she wades, into the unmown field, the shifting
dry grasses from which she'll emerge smelling of
herb and warm dust, with a deer tick crawling
across her brow. She will stay—indulgent
as I inspect her sun-warmed head and back, brush
away seeds and burrs and insects. Stay until
I kiss her nose. I have nothing to say really
about Boots, except that the sun speaks of her
on summer afternoons, and at the back of my eye
she waits—all shaggy grin and bad breath—
waits for me to come and sit and stay.

A Daughter Leaves Home

You're moving clear
across the country, your first
real job, with no idea even how
to sew on a button. Last of the packing
done, and you hold out a wool blazer,
the one we found together
in the designer section at Goodwill.
You make those pretty-please eyes
and my heart pricks—what else
have I neglected to teach you?
But with only a few minutes before you leave
for the airport, it's not the moment to say
If a powerful older man shows an intense personal interest...
If the subway entrance lights are out...

I reach for the button box, that tin reliquary
of jewel tones—twenty garnet
organza-covered shank buttons saved
from your prom dress, vegetable ivories from Peru
where every shop keeper pinched
your child-plump cheeks, basket-weave
leathers, antique brass—all sifting
through my fingers like sea glass.
I choose a circle of polished horn,
lick thumb and finger, roll the thread
to knot it tight.

No one ever taught me how
to sew on a button, either—
I'd poked and bled until my buttons held
and a messy row of thread-nests
dotted the backside of the fabric. Perhaps
this is just the way we learn
but I hope you'll simply watch a video
and sew your first one perfectly.
I do not say it—*world, world, please*
do not hurt her.

We sit together on the bed
while I line up the hole,
pierce the fabric
with a diamond-point needle,
pull it through and through again until
a black X marks the center.
Then I hold it out for you to fold.
I can see it's good to go,
good enough for a thousand fastenings,
a thousand unfastenings.

The Work

All October I watered the ground, tricking it
into believing the autumn rains had arrived.
Now there's half an acre of oxalis to be knifed
out of the dirt with my hori-hori.
Beautiful oxalis, sour on the tongue
and neon yellow in the fields. But invasive,
not meant for this garden of coastal scrub,
a refuge for over-wintering
monarchs, waxwings, turquoise bees.
What are the odds of keeping intact
a place of breathing and easy slumber?
I dig down to the corms—
those bulbus nodes of irrepressible
growth waiting in the deep to send up
yet another shoot, waiting out of sight.
Dirt finds its way beneath each fingernail,
into the cracks on my rough palms.
My basket fills with green leaves, with tender
white filaments laid side by side, thousands.

Balloon

By nature lighter
than air, I'm hungry
to chase galloping clouds
or shrink to a pinhead
in the blue riptide of sky.
Such a wonder then,
your hand
on the far end
of the tether. Astonishing
to find
I like it. The little tug
earthward
as the wind pulls
at the top of my head.
The line taut,
then slack then
finger-pressure danced—
my swaying pouch,
your shoes
patterning the pavement.
Look up I cry.
And you do. You do.

Ship Lights at Dawn

And lucky enough to wake one day in utter dark
the morning not yet born
        but on its way

to peer through the pane as the hard gleams
of fishing boat lanterns pinprick
        the black opacity of sky and sea,

to watch everything turn
to ghost gray pearl, a shift
        too gradual to register with the eye

yet suddenly all membranes melt
        borders dissipate and you,

you are afloat in a veiled world
with the now-soft lights of materializing ships
        drawing you to them.

Then the ship lights shine
        exactly the same as the light of the light

of the growing day you cannot hold,
        only let them

carry you like a boat like a prayer like a baby
        loosely moored and rocking.

Sea Urchin

You can spend a life like that—a creature
of tentacles and spikes holed up in a stone pit
of your own making. A compound eye
with a lid of pebbles to shutter the light.
Do you think I mean cramped or small? Listen.
What I see—O radiant punk
singing violence in the sunken garden—
how for decades you beam the purple rays
of your lantern, read the planktonic
stream written on cold pages:
*kelp, flea, fry, foam, larvae, louse. Bloom
or barren.* How without seeming to move,
you preside over the great untethering
of kelp forest columns, gnaw deeper
into rocks, and pluck the buzz from the still
pool at low tide. Even in death, shattered
and swallowed by sea otter, you violet
the bones of your enemy.

What the Ocean Dreams at Night

You are not a drop in the ocean. You are the entire ocean, in a drop.
—Rumi

How can I explain to you that one night
I lay face up on a bench beneath

rivers of stars and forgot about the sea
murmuring below me at the base of the cliff,

only breathed its rhythm,
the earth's pull, the moon's lift.

Can I tell you how the sea entered me—
unburdened of purpose, riddled

with travelers and hunters,
shadows and chandeliers spinning in its currents?

Though I am smaller than the smallest speck
in the largeness of galaxies and time,

I held an ocean
inside the cavity of my chest, in the glass vial

of my mind—sea, heaven, earth, porch.
And singing. There was

singing in the deep drifts, I tell you, singing.

Heirloom

Child's chair: sole survivor among
things touched by my grandmother.
The bent ash, soaked and rounded,
gleams where a girl's muslin dress
once rubbed. Scratches, where buttonhooked
shoes scuffed. Patina darkened to blood
mahogany, sweat silted into every divot.
The husband lost to German cavalry.
The daughter and two sons handed over
to strangers. The starting over.

How did it feel to watch my mother,
late child of a second marriage, run
her dimpled hand over the same ashwood
or tilt back on two legs and stress the frame?
To see the seat canes breached, re-woven.
Such fights, such marmalades and moths
this chair has weathered, yet it promenades
still, with a subtle bend in the foot,
plaiting light by my workroom window.

Hoshigaki

November and December, they hang from a wooden rod
    in my laundry room, sway eerily as tiny ghosts each time
the door is opened. Like shrunken heads, they shrivel
    and darken from succulent orange to leathery brown.

Eventually, they acquire a white, fuzzy bloom
    that people think is mold, though it is really
sugar that's found its way
    from the center of the fruit to the surface.

I remember old people like that—
    once-feisty great aunts and elderly third cousins
my father and I visited at Christmas, picking our way
    up icy, unshoveled stoops, as snow

dropped cold over the tops of our low boots.
    My father's gloved hand banged the storm door,
his breath misted the glass. The door would
    crack open to show one bifocaled eye,

then we would be inside a too-warm room and I flummoxed
    among cushions of graying chintz and stacks
of magazines until—with great delight—a rumpled elder
    offered me a cut-glass plate of stale Nabisco wafers

and dusty wrapped candy. Just as now, in the Christmas tradition,
    I set a board larded with brie, a block of honeycomb,
and slices of dried persimmon shaped like jigsaw puzzle pieces,
    then wait for a small child to take his first, uncertain bite.

Farewell-to-Spring

It's got a bloom that won't let go,
a bloom that hangs from a swollen capsule
long after losing its siren-pink flare.
A bloom that clings like an indecent widow
at an autumn funeral, tearing apart her clothes
even as she throws herself atop the wheeled casket
as it heads for the grave. The wind
can't axe that burgundy damask drape,
can't dislodge that moth-eaten flag
drooping at the top of its dried stem. My kind
of flower. One that says *if you want me
you're going to have to come get me*. In the season of seeds
and butterflies, I move through the meadow,
run my palms over each stalk,
leaving behind me a carpet of mottled
red and purple. When each pulled bloom detaches,
the top of the seed pod puckers its four lips—
goodbye and sweet goodbye.

Hidden Clock

Now the sooty shearwaters pull their day-long ribbon over the sea.
In the middle distance, the black thread of wings presses
along the invisible road of their ancestors, pulls us to the edge
of the water, to the edge of something we are trying to grasp.
There is the order of the world that we understand,
and the order of the world we do not understand.
A full moon always rises as the sun dissolves into the Pacific.
Wild blackberries are sweetest on the tongue of a small child.
There is no life to be had that doesn't include a knife stuck in the chest.
Now the hidden clock of our hungers folds its hands.
Feathers multiply on the shore. Squid shelter
among ocean ledges. A heart like the new moon—pitiless, unlit.

My Soul Refuses to Write Itself

Cuddles under the fake fur blanket. *No ideas but in things.*

Runs beside the car, a moon-faced dog refusing to be left behind.

Twig or light? What scratches at the window?

Woman-shaped room inside a violin, full of resin dust and a voice from a well.

That one note held and held, then quivered silence. Both true.

Hard bench under the big-leaf maple. The yellow carpet.

Stands my hair on end, electrical.

Slogs up the asphalt hill, sweat beads in the small of the back.

Props up its feet in the chapel ruins.

Says *Oh love, bring prosciutto and melon, sauvignon blanc.*

Soft Ground

Though I tell no one, I can hardly bear to leave the garden
even for one week. Perhaps that shows something lacking in me—

a fenced emotional life, an imagination hard as clay. The entire ride
to the airport, my chest tightens. Astonishing, how a person can be

changed entirely by the scent of sage and coyote mint,
by the quick tongues of painted ladies that swarm the sea daisies, by hours

of zigzagging bees, their back legs swinging. Am I a hermit now
in sun hat and rubber clogs, tracking rainfall and scribbling random
        observations?

But no—I am off! I am in the sky over the Pacific! Landless as an albatross.
Off, to bore indulgent hosts with my enthusiasm for rock swales and the
        migration

pattern of monarchs. For the bee at night, asleep inside the orange room
of a closed poppy. The swift sting of the solitary mud dauber, so docile
        usually,

until I kneel atop its burrow. Yes—I will bore you with enthusiasm
for the strange pleasure of tossing a dead mouse where the hawks and herons

can spy it. How in mere minutes, it disappears. I will be
inexplicable, in the manner of a foreigner. Most everywhere

is like that, now I have finally found a home. Seeds of blue-eyed grass
fall from their stalks into my palm. Weightless.

Notes

"Strange Gift" contains references to Emily Dickinson's *My life had stood — a Loaded Gun* [754] and the Joyce Carol Oates short story, "Ghost Girls."

"Home" contains descriptive language of tidepool life used in numerous online publications.

"Stealing Mulberries" takes its structure from the William Penn Warren poem, "Gold Glade."

"Field Notes" is loosely based on Jericho Brown's invented form, the duplex.

Acknowledgments

Some of these poems, or slightly different versions of them, have appeared in the journals and anthologies listed below. To the editors and staff of those journals, I am forever and profoundly grateful.

Alaska Quarterly Review: "The Work" (previously titled "Mercy")
Anacapa Review: "Stress Test"
Beloit Poetry Journal: "An Appreciation," "Strange Gift"
Crab Creek Review: "Morning Fog as Metaphor for Denial"
Cream City Review: "Despite the Usual Traffic"
Catamaran Literary Reader: "Balloon," "Truth"
Calyx: "Brogues"
DMQ Review: "Gift Set"
Entanglements: "To an Oxbow Lake"
Indiana Review: "Ship Lights at Dawn"
Lake Affect: "Beauty," "Sunday"
Mom Egg Review: "A Daughter Leaves Home," "Fragment"
New Ohio Review: "My Sister," "My Soul Refuses to Write Itself"
On the Seawall: "Bitter Greens," "Field Notes," "Hidden Clock," "Matisse at the National Gallery"
Phren-Z: "Stealing Mulberries"
Plume Poetry: "Received Wisdom"
Poet Lore: "Soft Ground," "Winter Wallop"
Radar Poetry: "Sea Urchin" "Stubborn"
Rattle Poetry: "Improvident"
RHINO Poetry: "Dear Thief," "Strata"
Rogue Agent: "Results Pending"
Rust & Moth: "Moon Garden"
Salamander: "Farewell to Spring"
Stone Gathering: (anthology) "Her Work," "Improvident," "Rutabagas" (reprints)
Swwim Every Day: "What We Heard"
Tar River Poetry: "Rutabagas"
The Inflectionist Review: "What the Ocean Dreams at Night"
The New Guard: "Pair of Eyes"
The Night Heron Barks: "As if to Waltz"
The Shore: "Her Work"

This Wandering State: Poems from Alta, vol. 2: "Improvident" (reprint)
Thrush Poetry: "Seeds"
Tinderbox Poetry Journal: "Home"
Valparaiso Review: "Heirloom," "Oysters"
West Trestle Review: "Apple Picking"
Whale Road Review: "Graphesthesia"

Gratitude

I am deeply grateful for the love and support of my family and friends, and of the amazing community of poets around me. I cannot imagine my life or my work without them.

I'd especially like to thank my teachers, Kim Addonizio, Sally Ashton, and Ellen Bass, and to acknowledge my poetry book club friends with whom I have been gathering and discussing poetry (and life) for nearly twenty years: Maureen Westenberger Bard, Susan Coons, Al Davis, Julie Jomo, Shonna Larson, Mary Powell, Joan Ragno, and Becky Schenone.

I owe a deep well of gratitude to the many poets who have read this manuscript or individual poems in the manuscript. Sarah Freligh and I were reading mates for many years that proved formative for me. Joan Kwon Glass helped me find a shape to the manuscript, and Danusha Lamerís has been unfailingly supportive. Thank you to Ellen Bass for generously spending time with this manuscript, and for bringing light and kindness to every conversation. Big thanks to my Santa Cruz area writer's group: Nancy Miller Gomez, Julie Murphy, and Cynthia White, and other poetry group members over many years: Kara Arguello, Jade Bradbury, Elaine Fletcher Chapman, Jessica Cohn, Kelly Cressio-Moeller, Hilary Rogers King, Catherine Latta, Nancy Meyer, Nancy Huxtable Mohr, Stephanie Pressman, and Marta Wallien.

Thank you to my daughter, Sophie, who created the cover image using a photo I had taken of a window in our cabin at the coast.

Finally, huge thanks to the folks at Wandering Aengus Press, for choosing my book and bringing it into the world: Jill McCabe Johnson, founder and publisher, and Tina Schumann, my editor.

About the Author

Veronica Kornberg splits her time between Portola Valley and Pescadero, a small town on the Central Coast of California. Recipient of the Morton Marcus Poetry Prize, and the 2025 Wandering Aengus Book Award in Poetry, her work has appeared in numerous journals, including *Alaska Quarterly Review*, *New Ohio Review*, *Poet Lore*, *Catamaran*, *Rattle*, *Indiana Review*, *Plume*, *Rhino Poetry*, *Calyx*, and *Beloit Poetry Journal*. Veronica co-founded a long-running poetry book club on the Peninsula, and is a Peer Reviewer for *Whale Road Review*. At home in Pescadero, you can find her happily exploring the tidepools, or on her knees in the dirt in her large habitat garden of coastal scrub. *Strange Gift* is her debut poetry collection. veronicakornberg.com

www.ingramcontent.com/pod-product-compliance
Lightning Source LLC
LaVergne TN
LVHW050029080526
838202LV00070B/6973